COLLECTED POEMS

PRIMO LEVI

Collected Poems

NEW EDITION

Translated by Ruth Feldman
and Brian Swann

faber and faber
LONDON · BOSTON

This paperback edition first published in Great Britain in 1988
by Faber and Faber Limited
3 Queen Square London WC1N 3AU
This new edition first published in 1992
Original Italian edition published as *Ad ora incerta*
by Garzanti Editore s.p.a. in Milan in 1984 and 1991

Photoset by Wilmaset Birkenhead Wirral
Printed in England by
Clays, St Ives plc
All rights reserved

A CIP record for this book
is available from the British Library

ISBN 0 571 16539 7

4 6 8 10 9 7 5

Contents

[v]

Note to Second Edition

Of the extra poems added to this edition, seventeen were published posthumously in Primo Levi's *Opere*, (Turin, Einaudi, 1989). Most of them had previously appeared in *La Stampa*, the Turin newspaper. 'Gedale's Song' comes from Levi's novel *Se Non Ora, Quando?* (Einaudi, 1982).

Acknowledgements

Grateful acknowledgement is made to the following publications in which some of the poems have appeared:
European Judaism, Granite, International Poetry Review, Jewish Currents, Jewish Quarterly, Mississippi Review, Partisan Review, Ploughshares, Poetry Review, Present Tense, Stand (England), *The Forward, The Jewish Advocate, The New Yorker, The Southern Review, Tikkun* and *Webster Review*.

'The Survivor' was used as the epigraph for *Moments of Reprieve*, Levi's concentration camp stories, translated by Ruth Feldman and published in the USA by Summit Books, Inc./Simon & Schuster and in the UK by Michael Joseph Ltd in 1986. 'Unfinished Business' was reprinted in *The Anthology of Magazine Verse*.

Translators' Preface

Primo Levi was born in Turin in 1919. As a young man, at the time of the persecution of Italian Jews, he joined a band of partisans but was soon captured, and in 1944 he was sent to the concentration camp called Buna-Monowitz, a subsidiary of Auschwitz, where his training as a chemist helped him to survive. The camp was liberated by the Russians in January 1945, and he finally made his way back to Italy after long wanderings. Following his retirement from the position of manager of a chemical factory in 1977, he devoted himself full time to writing. He died in Turin, on 11 April 1987.

Levi's first collection of poems, which was untitled, was printed privately by him for family and friends. These poems were eventually published in England by Menard Press with the title *Shemà* and won the John Florio Prize for best Italian to English translation. With some slight revision by Levi himself, they were included with his later poems in the volume *Ad ora incerta*, published by Garzanti Editore s.p.a. in Milan in 1984, and it is with their kind permission that we publish the translations. *Shemà* was translated by Ruth Feldman and Brian Swann. These poems are included in the Italian volume *Ad ora incerta*. The remaining poems in *Ad ora incerta* and the previously uncollected poems were translated by Ruth Feldman alone. 'Memorandum Book' ('Agenda' in Italian) was sent to Ruth Feldman by Levi subsequently in a letter and he approved its inclusion in the *Collected Poems*.

Shemà

Translated by Ruth Feldman and Brian Swann

Crescenzago

Perhaps you never thought of it
But the sun rises even at Crescenzago.
It rises, looks to see if there's a meadow,
A forest, a hill, a lake.
It doesn't find them, with an ugly face
Sucks vapors from the dry Naviglio.

The wind comes full tilt from the mountains,
Runs free over the endless plain.
But when it notices this smoke-stack
It veers and flies far off;
The smoke is so black and poisoned
The wind is afraid its breath will be cut off.

The old women sit using up the hours,
And count the falling rain.
The children's faces are the color
Of the streets' dead dust.
Here the women never sing,
But the tram whistles, raucous and constant.

At Crescenzago there's a window,
Behind which a girl is fading.
Needle and thread always in her right hand
She sews and mends, never stops looking at the clock.
When closing-time sounds
She sighs and weeps; this is the pattern of her life.

When the factory-whistle blows at dawn
They crawl out of their rumpled beds,
Go out into the street with their mouths full,
Circles under their eyes, ears ringing.
They pump up their bicycle tires,
Light half a cigarette.

From morning to night they keep
The grim black stonecrusher panting.
Or stand all day watching
The hand quiver on a dial.
They make love Saturday nights in the ditch
Next to the level-crossing keeper's house.

FEBRUARY 1943

Buna

Torn feet and cursed earth,
The long line in the gray morning.
The Buna smokes from a thousand chimneys,
A day like every other day awaits us.
The whistles terrible at dawn:
'You multitudes with dead faces,
On the monotonous horror of the mud
Another day of suffering is born.'
Tired companion, I see you in my heart.
I read your eyes, sad friend.
In your breast you carry cold, hunger, nothing.
You have broken what's left of the courage within you.
Colorless one, you were a strong man,
A woman walked at your side.
Empty companion who no longer has a name,
Forsaken man who can no longer weep,
So poor you no longer grieve,
So tired you no longer fear.
Spent once-strong man.
If we were to meet again
Up there in the world, sweet beneath the sun,
With what kind of face would we confront each other?

28 DECEMBER 1945

Singing

. . . But when we started singing
Those good foolish songs of ours,
Then everything was again
As it always had been.

A day was just a day,
And seven make a week.
Killing seemed an evil thing to us;
Dying – something remote.

The months pass rather quickly,
But there are still so many left!
Once more we were just young men:
Not martyrs, not infamous, not saints.

This and other things came into our minds
While we kept singing.
But they were cloudlike things,
Hard to explain.

3 JANUARY 1946

25 February 1944

I would like to believe in something,
Something beyond the death that undid you.
I would like to describe the intensity
With which, already overwhelmed,
We longed in those days to be able
To walk together once again
Free beneath the sun.

9 JANUARY 1946

The Crow's Song

'I came from very far away
To bring bad news.
I flew across the mountain,
Pierced the low cloud,
Mirrored my belly in the pond.
I flew without resting,
A hundred miles without resting,
To find your window,
To find your ear,
To bring you the sad tidings
That rob you of sleep's joy,
That taint your bread and wine,
Lodge every evening in your heart.'
    This is the way he sang, dancing, vicious,
    Beyond the glass, upon the snow.
    As he fell silent, he looked about, malign,
    Marked a cross on the ground with his beak,
    And opened his black wings wide.

9 JANUARY 1946

Shemà

You who live secure
In your warm houses,
Who return at evening to find
Hot food and friendly faces:

    Consider whether this is a man,
    Who labors in the mud
    Who knows no peace
    Who fights for a crust of bread
    Who dies at a yes or a no.
    Consider whether this is a woman,
    Without hair or name
    With no more strength to remember
    Eyes empty and womb cold
    As a frog in winter.

Consider that this has been:
I commend these words to you.
Engrave them on your hearts
When you are in your house, when you walk on your way,
When you go to bed, when you rise.
Repeat them to your children.
Or may your house crumble,
Disease render you powerless,
Your offspring avert their faces from you.

10 JANUARY 1946

Reveille

In the brutal nights we used to dream
Dense violent dreams,
Dreamed with soul and body:
To return; to eat; to tell the story.
Until the dawn command
Sounded brief, low:
    'Wstawać':
And the heart cracked in the breast.

Now we have found our homes again,
Our bellies are full,
We're through telling the story.
It's time. Soon we'll hear again
The strange command:
    'Wstawać'.

11 JANUARY 1946

Monday

Is anything sadder than a train
That leaves when it's supposed to,
That has only one voice,
Only one route?
There's nothing sadder.

Except perhaps a cart horse,
Shut between two shafts
And unable even to look sideways.
Its whole life is walking.

And a man? Isn't a man sad?
If he lives in solitude a long time,
If he believes time has run its course,
A man is a sad thing too.

17 JANUARY 1946

Another Monday

'I'll tell you who will end in Hell:
American journalists,
Teachers of mathematics,
Senators and sacristans.
Accountants, pharmacists
(If not all, the great majority),
Cats and financiers,
Company executives,
Those who get up early in the morning
When they don't have to.

Instead, those who will go to Paradise are:
Fishermen and soldiers,
Children, of course,
Horses and lovers,
Cooks and railroad men,
Russians and inventors,
Wine-tasters,
Charlatans and shoeshine boys,
Those who take the early morning tram
Yawning into their scarves.'
So Minos snarls horribly
From the megaphones of the Porta Nuova
Into the anguish of Monday morning
That must be experienced to be understood.

Avigliana, 28 JANUARY 1946

After R. M. Rilke

Lord, it's time; the wine is already fermenting.
The time has come to have a home,
Or to remain for a long time without one.
The time has come not to be alone,
Or else we will stay alone for a long time.
We will consume the hours over books,
Or in writing letters to distant places,
Long letters from our solitude.
And we will go back and forth through the streets,
Restless, while the leaves fall.

29 JANUARY 1946

Ostjuden

Our fathers of this earth,
Merchants of multiple skills,
Shrewd sages of the numerous progeny
God sowed across the world
As mad Ulysses sowed salt in the furrows:
I've found you everywhere,
Countless as the sea's sands,
You stiff-necked ones,
Poor tenacious human seed.

7 FEBRUARY 1946

Sunset at Fossoli

I know what it means not to return.
Through the barbed wire
I saw the sun go down and die.
I felt the words of the old poet
Tear at my flesh:
'Suns can go down and return.
For us, when the brief light is spent,
There is an unending night to be slept.'

7 FEBRUARY 1946

11 February 1946

I kept searching for you in the stars
When I questioned them as a child.
I asked the mountains for you,
But they gave me solitude and brief peace
Only a few times.
Because you weren't there, in the long evenings
I considered the rash blasphemy
That the world was God's error,
Myself an error in the world.
And when I was face to face with death –
No, I shouted from every fibre.
I hadn't finished yet;
There was still too much to do.
Because you were there before me,
With me beside you, just like today,
A man a woman under the sun.
I came back because you were there.

11 FEBRUARY 1946

The Glacier

We stopped, ventured a glance
Down the sad green jaws,
And the strength in our breasts dissolved
Like lost hope.
Within him a sad strength sleeps,
And when at night, in the silence
Of the moon, he sometimes shrieks and roars,
It is because, in his stone bed,
Huge sluggish dreamer,
He is struggling to turn over and cannot.

Avigliana, 15 MARCH 1946

The Witch

For a long time under the covers
She clasped the wax against her breast
Till it was soft and warm.
Then she got up, and with great pains
And with a patient loving hand,
Portrayed the living image
Of the man she carried in her heart.
When she was done, she threw the effigy on the fire
With leaves of grapevine, olive and oak,
So it would be consumed.

She felt herself dying from the pain
Because the spell had worked.
Only then could she cry.

Avigliana, 23 MARCH 1946

Avigliana

Heaven help the man who wastes the full moon
That comes only once a month.
Damn this town,
This stupid full moon
That shines placid and serene
Exactly as though you were with me.

. . . There is even a nightingale,
As in books of the last century.
But I made him fly away,
Far off, to the other side of the ditch:
It's all wrong for him to sing
While I am so alone.

I've left the fireflies alone
(There were lots of them all along the path),
Not because their name resembles yours,
But they are such gentle dear little creatures;
They make every care vanish.
And if someday we want to part,
And if someday we want to marry,
I hope the day will fall in June,
With fireflies all around
Like this evening, when you are not here.

28 JUNE 1946

Waiting

This is a time of lightning without thunder,
This is a time of unheard voices,
Of uneasy sleep and useless vigils.
Friend, do not forget the days
Of long easy silences,
Friendly nocturnal streets,
Serene meditations.
Before the leaves fall,
Before the sky closes again,
Before we are awakened again
By the familiar pounding of iron footsteps
In front of our doors.

2 JANUARY 1949

Epitaph

Oh you, passing by this hill – one
Among many – who mark this no longer solitary snow,
Hear my story. Stop for a few moments
Here where, dry-eyed, my comrades buried me,
Where, every summer, the gentle field-grass fed by me
Grows thicker and greener than elsewhere.
Killed by my companions for no small crime,
I, Micca the partisan, haven't lain here many years,
Hadn't lived many more when darkness struck.

Passer-by, I ask no pardon of you or any other,
No prayer or lament, no special remembrance.
Only one thing I beg: that this peace of mine endure,
That heat and cold succeed each other endlessly above me,
Without fresh blood filtering through clods
To reach me with its deadly warmth,
Waking to new pain these bones long turned to stone.

6 OCTOBER 1952

The Crow's Song II

'What is the number of your days? I've counted them:
Few and brief, each one weighted with care,
With anxiety about the inevitable night,
When nothing shields you from yourself;
With fear of the coming dawn,
Of my waiting, who wait for you,
Fear of me who (useless, useless to flee!)
Will follow you to the ends of the earth,
Astride your horse,
Staining the bridge of your ship
With my small black shadow,
Sitting at table where you sit,
Inevitable guest in all your refuges,
Constant companion of all your rests.

Until all that was foretold is done,
Until your strength dissolves,
Until you too end
Not with a clash but silently,
The way November trees are bared,
The way one finds a clock stopped.'

22 AUGUST 1953

[22]

There Were a Hundred

There were a hundred armed men.
When the sun rose in the sky,
They all took a step forward.
Hours passed, without a sound:
They never blinked.
When the bells rang,
They all moved a step forward.
So the day passed and it was evening.
But when the first star bloomed in the sky,
All together, they took a step forward.
'Get back, away from here, foul ghosts:
Go back to your old night.'
But no one answered, and instead,
All in a circle, they took a step forward.

1 MARCH 1959

For Adolf Eichmann

The wind runs free across our plains,
The live sea beats for ever at our beaches.
Man makes earth fertile, earth gives him flowers and fruits.
He lives in toil and joy; he hopes, fears, begets sweet
    offspring.

. . . And you have come, our precious enemy,
Forsaken creature, man ringed by death.
What can you say now, before our assembly?
Will you swear by a god? What god?
Will you leap happily into the grave?
Or will you at the end, like the industrious man
Whose life was too brief for his long art,
Lament your sorry work unfinished,
The thirteen million still alive?

Oh son of death, we do not wish you death.
May you live longer than anyone ever lived.
May you live sleepless five million nights,
And may you be visited each night by the suffering of
    everyone who saw,
Shutting behind him, the door that blocked the way back,
Saw it grow dark around him, the air fill with death.

20 JULY 1960

Landing

Happy the man who has made harbor,
Who leaves behind him seas and storms,
Whose dreams are dead or never born,
And who sits and drinks in a Bremen beer-hall,
Beside the stove, in peace and quiet.
Happy the man like an extinguished flame,
Happy the man like estuary sand,
Who has laid down his load and wiped his forehead
And rests at the side of the road.
He fears nothing, hopes for nothing, expects nothing,
But stares fixedly at the setting sun.

10 SEPTEMBER 1964

Lilith

Lilith, our second kinswoman,
Created by God with the same clay
That served for Adam.
Lilith lives in the middle of the undertow,
But emerges at the new moon
And flies restless through the snowy nights,
Irresolute between earth and sky.
She spins around in circles,
Rustles unexpected against the windows
Where newborn babies sleep.
She hunts them out and tries to kill them.
Therefore you will hang over their beds
The medallion with the three words.
But everything she does is useless: all her desires.
She coupled with Adam, after the sin,
But the only things born of her
Are spirits without bodies or peace.
It is written in the great book
That she is a beautiful woman down to the waist.
The rest is will-o'-the-wisp and pale light.

25 MAY 1965

In the Beginning

Fellow humans, to whom a year is a long time,
A century a venerable goal,
Struggling for your bread,
Tired, fretful, tricked, sick, lost:
Listen, and may it be mockery and consolation.
Twenty billion years before now,
Brilliant, soaring in space and time,
There was a ball of flame, solitary, eternal,
Our common father and our executioner.
It exploded, and every change began.
Even now the thin echo of this one reverse catastrophe
Resounds from the farthest reaches.
From that one spasm everything was born:
The same abyss that enfolds and challenges us,
The same time that spawns and defeats us,
Everything anyone has ever thought,
The eyes of every woman we have loved,
Suns by the thousands
And this hand that writes.

13 AUGUST 1970

Via Cigna

There isn't a shabbier street in this whole city.
Fog and night; shadows on the sidewalk
Crossed by the gleam of traffic-lights
As though sodden with nothing, clots
Of nothing, really our counterparts.
Maybe the sun no longer exists.
Maybe it will be dark for ever. Yet
On other nights the Pleiades smiled.
Maybe this is the eternity awaiting us:
Not the Father's bosom, but clutch,
Brake, clutch, shifting to low gear,
Maybe eternity is traffic-lights.
Maybe it was better to squander life
In one short night, like a drone.

2 FEBRUARY 1973

The Black Stars

Let no one sing again of love or war.

The order from which the cosmos took its name has been
   dissolved;
The heavenly legions are a tangle of monsters,
The universe – blind, violent and strange – assails us.
The sky is strewn with horrible dead suns,
Dense sediments of mangled atoms.
Only desperate heaviness emanates from them,
Not energy, not messages, not particles, not light.
Light itself falls back down, broken by its own weight,
And all of us human seed, we live and die for nothing,
The skies perpetually revolve in vain.

30 NOVEMBER 1974

Leavetaking

It has grown late, my friends.
So I won't accept bread or wine from you,
Only some hours of silence,
The tales of Peter the fisherman,
The musky perfume of this lake,
The ancient scent of burnt twigs,
The gossipy screeching of gulls,
The lichens' free gold on roof-tiles,
And a bed, in which to sleep alone.
In exchange, I'll leave you *nebbich* poems like these
Made to be read by five or six readers.
Then we'll go off, each intent on his own cares,
Since, as I was saying, it has grown late.

Anguillara, 28 DECEMBER 1974

At an Uncertain Hour

Translated by Ruth Feldman

Pliny

Don't hold me back, friends, let me set out.
I won't go far; just to the other shore.
I want to observe at close hand that dark cloud,
Shaped like a pine tree, rising above Vesuvius,
And find the source of this strange light.
Nephew, you don't want to come along? Fine; stay here
    and study.
Recopy the notes I gave you yesterday.
You needn't fear the ash; ash on top of ash.
We're ash ourselves; remember Epicurus?
Quick, get the boat ready, it is already night:
Night at midday, a portent never seen before.
Don't worry, sister, I'm cautious and expert;
The years that bowed me haven't passed in vain.
Of course I'll come back quickly. Just give me time
To ferry across, observe the phenomena and return,
Draw a new chapter from them tomorrow
For my books, that will, I hope, still live
When for centuries my old body's atoms
Will be whirling, dissolved in the vortices of the universe,
Or live again in an eagle, a young girl, a flower.
Sailors, obey me: launch the boat into the sea.

23 MAY 1978

The Girl-Child of Pompei

Since everyone's anguish is our own,
We live yours over again, thin child,
Clutching your mother convulsively
As though, when the noon sky turned black,
You wanted to re-enter her.
To no avail, because the air, turned poison,
Filtered to find you through the closed windows
Of your quiet thick-walled house,
Once happy with your song, your timid laugh.
Centuries have passed, the ash has petrified
To imprison those delicate limbs for ever.
In this way you stay with us, a twisted plaster cast,
Agony without end, terrible witness to how much
Our proud seed matters to the gods.
Nothing is left of your far-removed sister,
The Dutch girl imprisoned by four walls
Who wrote of her youth without tomorrows.
Her silent ash was scattered by the wind,
Her brief life shut into a crumpled notebook.
Nothing remains of the Hiroshima schoolgirl,
A shadow printed on a wall by the light of a thousand suns,
Victim sacrificed on the altar of fear.
Powerful of the earth, masters of new poisons,
Sad secret guardians of final thunder,
The torments heaven sends us are enough.
Before your finger presses down, stop and consider.

20 NOVEMBER 1978

[34]

Huayna Capac

Huayna Capac, Inca emperor, died in 1527, shortly after Francisco Pizarro's first landing at Tumbes. It is said that one of his messengers supped on board the Spanish ship, and that Huayna Capac, by then a dying man, had had news of the strangers' arrival.

Heaven help you, messenger, if you lie to your old
   sovereign.
There are no ships like the ones you are describing,
Bigger than my royal palace, driven by the storm.
Those dragons you rave about, bronze-sheathed,
Gleaming, with silver feet, do not exist.
There are no bearded warriors; they're ghosts.
Waking or sleeping, your mind invented them,
Or maybe a god sent them to deceive you.
That often happens in calamitous times
When old certainties lose their outlines,
Virtues are negated, and faith fades.
The red plague doesn't come from them; it was already
   there.
It's not a portent, not an ill omen.
I shan't listen to you. Gather your servants and depart.
Descend through the valley, rush across the plain,
Thrust your sceptre among your enemy half-brothers,
Sons of my vigor, Huascar and Atahualpa.
Stop the war that bloodies my kingdom
So the cunning stranger won't profit by it.
He asked for gold? Give him a hundredweight,
A thousand. If hate has split this empire of the Sun,
The gold will inject hate into the other half of the world,
There where the intruder cradles his monsters.
Give him the Inca gold. It will be the happiest of gifts.

8 DECEMBER 1978

[35]

The Gulls of Settimo

From meander to meander, year by year,
The lords of the sky have come up the river,
Along the banks, up from its violent mouths.
They have forgotten surf and salt water,
The crafty patient hunts, voracious crabs.
Up through Crespino, Polesella, Ostiglia,
The newborn more determined than the old,
Beyond Luzzara, beyond dead Viadana,
Greedy for our ignoble refuse,
Fatter from bend to bend.
They have explored Caorso's mists,
The lazy branches between Cremona and Piacenza.
Borne on the superhighway's tepid breath,
Mournfully shrieking their brief greeting,
They have paused at the Ticino's mouth,
Built nests under Valenza's bridge
Among tar-clots and polyethylene scraps.
They've sailed to the mountain, beyond Casale and
    Chivasso,
Fleeing the sea and lured by our abundance.
Now they hover restlessly above Settimo Torinese,
And, forgetful of the past, ransack our rubbish.

9 APRIL 1979

Annunciation

Don't be dismayed, woman, by my fierce form.
I come from far away, in headlong flight;
Whirlwinds may have ruffled my feathers.
I am an angel, yes, and not a bird of prey;
An angel, but not the one in your paintings
That descended in another age to promise another Lord.
I come to bring you news, but wait until my heaving chest,
The loathing of the void and dark, subside.
Sleeping in you is one who will destroy much sleep.
He's still unformed but soon you'll caress his limbs.
He will have the gift of words, the fascinator's eyes,
Will preach abomination and be believed by all.
Jubilant and wild, singing and bleeding,
They'll follow him in bands, kissing his footprints.
He will carry the lie to the farthest borders.
Evangelize with blasphemy and the gallows.
He'll rule in terror, suspect poisons
In spring-water, in the air of high plateaus.
He'll see deceit in the clear eyes of the newborn,
And die unsated by slaughter, leaving behind sown hate.
This is your growing seed. Woman, rejoice.

22 JUNE 1979

Toward the Valley

The carts plod toward the valley,
Brushwood smoke stagnates, bitter and blue,
A last bee uselessly plumbs the meadow saffron;
Slow, swollen with water, landslides crash down.
Mist rises quickly among the larches, as though
    summoned:
I've followed it in vain, my steps flesh-heavy;
It will soon fall again as rain: the season is over.
Our half of the world travels toward winter.
All our seasons will soon end.
How long will these sound limbs continue to obey me?
It's late for living, late for loving,
For fathoming the sky, understanding the world.
It's time to go down
Toward the valley, our faces closed and mute,
To shelter in the shadow of our cares.

5 SEPTEMBER 1979

Wooden Heart

My next-door neighbor is robust;
It's a horse-chestnut tree in Corso Re Umberto:
My age but doesn't look it.
It harbors sparrows and blackbirds, isn't ashamed,
In April, to put forth buds and leaves,
Fragile flowers in May,
And in September burrs, prickly but harmless,
With shiny tannic chestnuts inside.
An impostor but naive: it wants people to believe
It rivals its fine mountain brother,
Lord of sweet fruits and precious mushrooms.
A hard life: every five minutes its roots
Are trampled by streetcars Nos. 8 and 19;
Deafened by noise, it grows twisted,
As though it would like to leave this place.
Year after year, it sucks slow poisons
From the methane-soaked subsoil,
Is watered with dog urine.
The wrinkles in its bark are clogged
With the avenue's septic dust.
Under the bark hang dead chrysalises
That never will be butterflies.
Still, in its sluggish wooden heart
It feels, savors the seasons' return.

10 MAY 1980

The First Atlas

Abysmal Abyssinia, iridescent irate Ireland,
Steely blue Sweden,
Finland, finishing-point of every land,
Poland close to the Pole, the pale color of snow.
Angular Mongoloid Mongolia,
Fast-coursing Corsica, index finger pointed
At Liguria's sucked-in corsair belly.
Argentina jingling with silver bells
Hung on the necks of thousands of argent cows,
Freedom-hungry Hungary, brown gob of goulash.
Intriguing Italy, boot with misshapen heel.
Ancona, black abscess halfway up the calf.
Blood-red Bolivia, land of stamps,
Germany, dark blue country of germs and buds,
Fringed Greece, pendulous udder
Surrounded by countless squirts of rosy milk.
Undaunted England, austere, witty lame lady,
Wild and proud of her plumed bonnet.
Black Sea, a brooding cat, Sea of Azov its kitten,
Baltic Sea praying, kneeling on ice,
Caspian Sea, a bear dancing on marsh mud.
Toxic Tuscany, overturned pot, its handle
Stuck in the brown of a Tuscan cigar.
Cynical oblique China printed on yellow silk
Shut in the great wall of bright China ink,
Panama of well-glued twisted straw hats.

Uruguay Paraguay: twin parrots,
Africa South America, ugly iron spears
Poised to threaten no one's Antarctic.

Not one of the lands written into your destiny
Will speak to you the language of your first Atlas.

28 JUNE 1980

12 July 1980

Have patience, my weary lady,
Patience with worldly things,
With your companions on the journey, myself included,
From the moment I fell to your lot.
Accept, after all these years, a few crabbèd lines
For your well-rounded birthday.
Have patience, my impatient lady,
So ground down, mortified, flayed,
You who flay yourself a little every day
So that the naked flesh hurts you still more.
It is no longer the time to live alone.
Accept, to please me, these fourteen lines.
They are my rough way of saying how dear you are,
And that I wouldn't be in this world without you.

12 JULY 1980

Dark Band

Could one choose a more absurd route?
In Corso San Martino there's an anthill
Half a yard from the streetcar tracks,
Right where the wheels grind by.
A long dark band unravels:
One ant comes face to face with another,
Maybe to spy out the way, their chances.
In short, these stupid sisters,
Super-industrious, stubborn, mad,
Have dug their city right in ours,
Traced their track on top of ours.
They scurry about there, unsuspecting,
Tireless in their tenuous affairs,
Paying no heed to
       I don't want to write it,
I don't want to write about this band,
Don't want to write about any dark band.

13 AUGUST 1980

Autobiography

'Once I was already youth and maid, bush, bird, and mute fish
that leaps out of the sea.'

(from a fragment by Empedocles)

I who speak to you am old as the world.
In the darkness of the beginnings
I swarmed through the sea's blind pits,
Blind myself, but already yearning for light
When I still lay in the rotting depths.
I gulped salt with a thousand tiny throats;
I was a fish, slimy and swift. I eluded snares,
Showed my offspring the crab's tortuous paths.
Higher than a tower, I outraged the sky;
The mountains trembled at the shock of my passing.
My brute bulk obstructed valleys:
Your rocks still bear today
The incredible impress of my scales.
I sang to the moon the toad's liquid song,
My constant hunger riddled wood.
An impetuous timid deer, I ran through woods
That are ash today, pleased by my strength.
I was drunken cicada, shrewd dread tarantula,
Salamander, scorpion, unicorn and asp.
I suffered whipping, heat,
Cold, the desperation of the yoke,
The donkey's silent vertigo on the treadmill.
I was a maiden, hesitating in the dance;
Surveyor, I probed the secret of the circle,
The dubious paths of clouds and winds.

I have known tears and laughter and much beauty.
Therefore, don't mock me, men of Agrigento,
If this old body is deeply and strangely marked.

12 NOVEMBER 1980

Voices

Voices mute for ever, or since yesterday, or just stilled;
If you listen hard you can still catch the echo.
Hoarse voices of those who can no longer speak,
Voices that speak and can no longer say anything,
Voices that think they're saying something,
Voices that speak and can't be understood:
Choruses and cymbals for smuggling sense
Into a senseless message.
Pure hubbub to pretend
That silence is not silence.
A vous parle, compaings de galle:
I speak to you, companions of revelry,
Drunk like me on words,
Sword-words, poison-words,
Key-words, lockpicker-words,
Salt-words, mask and nepenthe.
The place we're going to is silent
Or deaf. It's the limbo of the lonely and the deaf.
      You'll have to run the last lap deaf,
      You'll have to run the last lap by yourself.

10 FEBRUARY 1981

Unfinished Business

Sir, starting next month,
Please accept my resignation
And, if necessary, find a replacement for me.
I leave a lot of uncompleted work,
Either from laziness or practical problems.
I should have said something to someone,
But no longer know what or to whom. I have forgotten.
I should have given something away, too:
A word of wisdom, a gift, a kiss.
I've put it off from one day to the next. Forgive me.
I'll take care of it in the short time that's left.
I have, I fear, neglected important clients.
I should have visited
Faraway cities, islands, deserted lands;
You'll have to cross them off the program
Or entrust them to my successor's care.
I should have planted trees and haven't done it,
Built myself a house,
Perhaps not beautiful but conforming to a plan.
Above all, dear sir, I had in mind
A marvelous book that would have
Revealed innumerable secrets,
Alleviated pain and fear,
Dissolved doubts, given to many people
The boon of tears and laughter.
You'll find the outline in my drawer,
In back, with the unfinished business.
I haven't had time to see it through. Too bad.
It would have been a fundamental work.

19 APRIL 1981

[47]

Partisan

Where are you now, partisans of all the valleys:
Tarzan, Riccio, Sparviero, Saetta, Ulisse?
Many sleep in decorous graves;
Those who are left are white-haired
And tell the sons of sons how,
In the remote time of certainties,
They broke the Germans' siege
There where the chairlift is now.
Some buy and sell land,
Others nibble at their pensions from the INPS,
Or grow wrinkled at the local council meetings.
On your feet, old men: for us there's no discharge.
Let's find each other again. Let's go back to the mountains,
Slow, breathless, with stiff knees,
With many winters in our backbones.
The steep path will be difficult for us,
Hard the cot and hard the bread.
We'll look and not know one another,
Mistrustful, peevish and touchy.
Like then, we will stand guard
So the enemy will not take us by surprise at dawn.
What enemy? Every man is the enemy of every other,
With everyone split by an inner border,
The right hand enemy of the left.
On your feet, old men, enemies of yourselves:
Our war is never over.

23 JULY 1981

Arachne

Patience! I'll weave myself another web.
My patience is long, my mind is short;
Eight legs and a hundred eyes,
But a thousand spinner breasts.
I don't like fasting;
I like flies and males.
I'll rest for four days, seven,
Holed up in my lair,
Until I feel my abdomen heavy
With fine shiny, sticky thread.
And I'll weave myself another web,
Like the one you tore when you passed by,
According to the plan printed
On my memory's tiny tape.
I'll seat myself in the center
And wait till a male arrives,
Wary but drunk with desire,
To fill my belly and my womb
At one fell swoop.
Nimble and fierce, as soon as it gets dark,
Quickly, quickly, knot upon knot,
I'll weave myself another web.

29 OCTOBER 1981

2000

A thousand plus a thousand: a winning-post,
A thread of white wool, no longer that far off,
Or maybe black or red. Who could say?
It's unlucky to know. To try to question
The numbers of Babylon is not permissible.

11 JANUARY 1982

Passover

Tell me: how is this night different
From all other nights?
How, tell me, is this Passover
Different from other Passovers?
Light the lamp, open the door wide
So the pilgrim can come in,
Gentile or Jew;
Under the rags perhaps the prophet is concealed.
Let him enter and sit down with us;
Let him listen, drink, sing and celebrate Passover;
Let him consume the bread of affliction,
The Paschal Lamb, sweet mortar and bitter herbs.
This is the night of differences
In which you lean your elbow on the table,
Since the forbidden becomes prescribed,
Evil is translated into good.
We will spend the night recounting
Far-off events full of wonder,
And because of all the wine
The mountains will skip like rams.
Tonight they exchange questions:
The wise, the godless, the simple-minded and the child.
And time reverses its course,
Today flowing back into yesterday,
Like a river enclosed at its mouth.
Each of us has been a slave in Egypt,
Soaked straw and clay with sweat,
And crossed the sea dry-footed.
You too, stranger.

This year in fear and shame,
Next year in virtue and in justice.

9 APRIL 1982

[52]

Laid Up

Alone among the many new ones, an old keel,
Sticky, iridescent with oil,
Rocks sluggishly on the harbor water.
Its wood is leprous, the iron tawny with rust.
The plating bumps hollowly against the wharf.
Fat as a belly pregnant with nothing.
Under the water's surface
You see soft seaweed, the slow augurs
Of teredos and stubborn barnacles.
On the scorching cover, white spots
Of calcined gull droppings,
Tar oxidized by sun, and useless paint,
Brown spots of human excrement, I'm afraid,
And spiderwebs of salt. I never knew that there
Were spiders too, nesting on laid-up boats.
What prey they hope for, I don't know, but they
Probably know what they're about.
The rudder creaks and lazily obeys
The secret caprices of light currents.
On the stern, already familiar with the world,
A name and motto now illegible.
Instead the mooring rope of red
And yellow nylon, shiny and taut, is new,
Just in case the mad old lady
Gets a notion to set out to sea again.

27 JUNE 1982

[53]

Old Mole

What's strange about it? I didn't like the sky,
So chose to live alone and in the dark.
My hands were made for digging,
Concave, hooked, but sensitive and tough.
Now I travel, sleepless,
Imperceptible under the meadows,
Where I feel neither cold nor heat,
Nor wind rain day night snow,
Where eyes are of no more use to me.
I dig and find succulent roots,
Tubers, rotten wood, mushroom filaments,
And if a boulder blocks my path
I go around it, laboriously but unhurried,
Because I'm always sure of where I want to go.
I find earthworms, larvae, salamanders,
At times a truffle,
At others a viper – a fine meal –
And treasures buried by who knows whom.
In earlier days I followed female moles,
And when I heard one scratching,
Dug my way toward her.
No more. If it happens now, I change direction.
But when the moon is new I get excited.
Then, sometimes I amuse myself
By suddenly popping out to frighten dogs.

22 SEPTEMBER 1982

A Bridge

It's not like other bridges,
That stand up under centuries of snow
So herds can go in search of food and water,
Or celebrants can pass from place to place.
This is a different kind of bridge,
Pleased if you stop halfway across
To take deep soundings, ask yourself
If you can count on being alive next day.
It is alive in a deadened way,
And is never granted peace,
Perhaps because from its pilaster's hollow
The slow poison filters of an old
And evil spell I shan't describe.
Or perhaps, as nightwatchers used to tell,
Because it's the fruit of a wicked pact.
Therefore, here you will never see the current
Quietly reflecting the bridge's span,
But only crinkled waves and eddying whirlpools.
Therefore it polishes itself in sand,
Stone keeps on grating against stone,
And it presses presses presses against the riverbanks
In order to crack the earth's crust.

25 NOVEMBER 1986

The Work

There now, it's finished: there's no more to be done.
How heavy the pen's weight in my hand!
It was so light a little while ago,
Lively as quicksilver.
All I had to do was follow it;
It guided my hand
The way a sighted person guides a blind one,
The way a woman leads you to the dance.
Now that's enough, the work is finished,
Polished, spherical.
If you removed so much as a word
You'd leave a hole that oozes serum.
If you should add one, it would
Stick out like an ugly wart.
Change one and it would jar
Like a dog howling at a concert.
What to do now? How to detach yourself?
With every work that's born you die a little.

15 JANUARY 1983

A Mouse

A mouse got in, from some hole or other,
Not silent, as they usually are, but
Presumptuous, arrogant and bombastic.
A talky sententious equestrian,
It climbed to my bookcase top
And preached to me,
Quoting Plutarch, Nietzsche and Dante:
That I must not waste time,
Blah, blah, that time is growing short,
Lost time never comes back,
And time is money. That the man
Who has time, had better not wait for time
Because life is brief and art is long,
And at my back it seems to hear
Some winged curved chariot hurrying near.
What impudence! What conceit!
I really was fed up.
As if a mouse knows what time is!
It's the one who's making me waste time
With its bold-faced scolding.
It's a mouse, right? Let it go preach to mice.
I told it to get lost:
I know too well what time is.
It's part of lots of physics equations,
Squared in some cases,
Or with a negative exponent.
I can look after myself;
I don't need anyone else to run my life.
Prima caritas incipit ab ego.

15 JANUARY 1983

[57]

Nachtwache

'Watchman, what of the night?'

'I've heard the owl repeat
Its hollow prescient note,
The bat shriek at its hunting,
The water-snake rustle
Under the pond's soaked leaves.
I have heard vinous voices,
Stammering, angry, as I drowsed
In the tavern near the chapel.
I have heard lovers' whispers, laughter,
And the labored breathing of absolved longings,
Adolescents murmuring in their dreams,
Others tossing, sleepless from desire.
I've seen silent heat-lightning,
The terror every night
Of the girl who lost her way
And doesn't know bed from coffin.
I've heard the hoarse panting
Of a lonely old man struggling with death,
A woman torn in labor,
The cry of a just-born child.
Stretch out and sleep, citizen.
Everything is in order; this night is half over.'

10 AUGUST 1983

[58]

Agave

Neither useful nor beautiful,
I boast no pleasing colors or scents;
My roots eat into cement.
My thorn-edged leaves,
Sword-sharp, protect me.
I'm mute, speak only my plant language,
An outmoded tongue
Hard for you, man, to understand.
Exotic, since I come from far away,
From a cruel country
Full of poisons, volcanoes, wind.
I've waited many years to send up
My towering desperate flower,
Ugly, wooden, stiff, but stretching toward the sky.
It's our way of shouting:
I'll die tomorrow. Now do you understand?

10 SEPTEMBER 1983

Pearl Oyster

You – hotblooded, hasty, coarse –
What do you know of these soft limbs of mine
Except their flavor? And yet
They feel both cold and warmth,
And, deep in the water, the impure and the pure.
They contract and relax, obedient
To intimate mute rhythms,
And, quick-moving stranger, they enjoy food,
Cry out in hunger like your limbs.
If, walled between my stony valves,
I had memory and intelligence like you,
And cemented to my rock, I divined the sky?
I'm more like you than you imagine,
Condemned to secrete, secrete
Tears, sperm, mother-of-pearl and pearls.
Like you, if a splinter injures my mantle,
Day after day I cover it over silently.

30 SEPTEMBER 1983

The Snail

Why hurry when you're so well defended?
Is one place really better than another
Provided there's no lack of moisture and of grass?
Why run and risk adventures when all you need
Is to close tightly to have peace?
Then, if the universe turns hostile,
You can seal yourself silently
Behind your white limestone covering,
Deny the world, and deny yourself to it.
But when the meadow's drenched with dew,
Or rain has soothed the ground,
Each path is your highway,
Paved with fine shiny slime,
A bridge from leaf to leaf, and stone to stone.
You navigate with care, secret and sure,
Sound out the way with telescopic eyes,
Graceful, repugnant, logarithmic.
There: you've found your mate,
And, fearfully, strained
And pulsing out of your shell,
You savor the shy delights of dubious loves.

7 DECEMBER 1983

[61]

A Profession

All you need to do is wait, fountain pen ready:
The lines will whir round you, like drunken moths.
One comes to the flame and you snatch it.
To be sure, you're not finished; one isn't enough.
Still it's a lot – the beginning of your task.
The others rival one another to light nearby,
In a row or a circle, order or disorder,
Simple and quiet and slaves to your command.
You are the master – no doubt about it.
If it's a good day, you line them up.
Fine work, isn't it? Time-honored,
Sixty centuries old and always new,
With fixed or slack rules,
Or no rules at all, just as you like.
You feel you're in good company,
Not lazy, lost, or always useless,
Sandaled and togaed, cloaked
In fine linen, with your degree.
Just take nothing for granted.

2 JANUARY 1984

Flight

Rock and sand and no water:
Sand stitched by his countless steps
All the way to the horizon.
He was fleeing, and no one was following.
Gravel trampled and worn,
Stone gnawed by the wind,
Split by successive frosts;
Dry wind and no water.
No water for him
Whose only need was water,
Water to erase,
Water fierce dream,
Impossible water to cleanse himself again.
Leaden sun without rays,
Sky and dunes and no water.
Ironic water feigned by mirages;
Precious water drained off in sweat.
And overhead, unreachable,
The water of cirrus clouds.

    He found the well and descended,
Plunged his hands in and the water turned red.
No one could ever drink there again.

12 JANUARY 1984

The Survivor

to B.V.

Dopo di allora, ad ora incerta,
Since then, at an uncertain hour,
That agony returns:
And till my ghastly tale is told,
This heart within me burns.

Once more he sees his companions' faces
Livid in the first faint light,
Gray with cement dust,
Nebulous in the mist,
Tinged with death in their uneasy sleep.
At night, under the heavy burden
Of their dreams, their jaws move,
Chewing a nonexistent turnip.
'Stand back, leave me alone, submerged people,
Go away. I haven't dispossessed anyone,
Haven't usurped anyone's bread.
No one died in my place. No one.
Go back into your mist.
It's not my fault if I live and breathe,
Eat, drink, sleep and put on clothes.'

4 FEBRUARY 1984

The Elephant

Dig and you'll find my bones,
Absurd in this snow-filled place.
I was tired of marching and heavy loads;
I missed the warmth and grass.
You'll find coins and Punic weapons
Buried by avalanches: absurd, absurd!
Absurd my story and that of History.
What were Carthage and Rome to me?
Now my fine ivory, our pride and joy,
Noble, curved like the crescent moon,
Lies splintered among the river's stones.
It wasn't made for piercing breastplates
But for digging up roots and pleasing females.
We fight only for mates,
Wisely, without bloodshed.
Would you like to hear my story? It's brief.
The cunning Indian trapped and tamed me,
The Egyptian shackled and sold me,
The Phoenician covered me with armor
And set a tower on my back.
It was absurd that I, a tower of flesh,
Invulnerable, gentle and terrible,
Forced here among these enemy mountains,
Slipped on your ice I'd never seen before.
When one of us falls down, there is no saving him.
A bold blind man tried for a long time
To find my heart with his lance-point.

I've hurled my useless dying trumpeting
At these peaks,
Livid in the sunset: 'Absurd, absurd.'

                                    23 MARCH 1984

[66]

Sidereus Nuncius

I have seen two-horned Venus
Travelling gently in the sky.
I have seen valleys and mountains on the Moon,
Saturn with its three bodies;
I, Galileo, first among humans,
Have seen four stars circle round Jupiter,
The Milky Way split into
Countless legions of new worlds.
I have seen, unbelieved, ominous spots
Foul the Sun's face.
This spyglass was made by me,
A man of learning but with clever hands;
I've polished its lenses, aimed it at the Heavens
As you would aim a bombard.
I am the one who broke open the Sky
Before the Sun burned my eyes.

    Before the Sun burned my eyes
    I had to stoop to saying
    I did not see what I saw.
    The one who bound me to the earth
    Did not unleash earthquakes or lightning.
    His voice was subdued and smooth;
    He had the face of everyman.
    The vulture that gnaws me every evening
    Has everyman's face.

11 APRIL 1984

Give Us

Give us something to destroy:
A corolla, a silent corner,
A boon companion, a magistrate,
A telephone booth,
A journalist, a renegade,
A fan of the opposing team,
A lamp-post, a man-hole cover, a bench.
Give us something to deface:
A plaster wall, the Mona Lisa,
A mudguard, a tombstone.
Give us something to rape:
A timid girl,
A flower-bed, ourselves.
Don't despise us; we're heralds and prophets.
Give us something that burns, offends, cuts, smashes,
    fouls,
And makes us feel that we exist.
Give us a club or a Nagant,
Give us a syringe or a Suzuki.
Pity us.

                                        30 APRIL 1984

[68]

Chess

Only my enemy for all time,
The abominable black queen,
Has had nerve equal to mine
In helping her inept king.
Inept and cowardly mine too – that's understood.
From the very start he crouched
Behind his row of plucky pawns,
Then fled across the chessboard,
Askew, absurd, with little stumbling steps.
Battles are not for kings.
But I!
If I had not been there!
Rooks and horses, yes, but I!
Powerful and ready, upright and diagonal,
Far-reaching as a catapult,
I pierced their defenses.
They had to bow their heads,
The fraudulent, haughty black ones.
Victory intoxicates like a wine.

Now it's all over,
The skill and hatred are spent.
A mighty hand has swept us away,
Weak and strong, cautious, wise and mad,
Whites and blacks every which way, lifeless.
Then, with a clatter of gravel, it threw us
Into the black wooden box
And closed the lid.
When will we play again?

9 MAY 1984

[69]

Chess II

You mean that, halfway through,
With the game all but over, you'd like
To change the rules of play?
You know perfectly well it's not allowed.
To castle under threats?
Or go so far, if I am not mistaken,
As to replay the moves you made when you began?
Come on! You too accepted these rules
When you sat down at the chessboard.
A piece touched is a piece moved:
Ours is a serious game. No bargaining.
And no confusion; no cheating allowed.
Move! You haven't much time left.
Don't you hear the clock ticking away?
In any case, why not give up?
To foresee my plays,
Greater knowledge than yours is needed.
You knew right from the start
I was the stronger of the two.

23 JUNE 1984

Memorandum Book

In such a night as this,
Of north wind and rain mixed with snow,
There is someone who drowses in front of a TV,
Someone who resolves to rob a bank.
In such a night as this,
Distant as it takes light to travel in five days,
There is a comet that plummets onto us
From the black womb without height or depth.
The same one Giotto painted,
It will bring neither luck nor disasters,
But ancient ice and a reply, perhaps.
In such a night as this
There is a half-mad old man,
Fine metalworker in his day,
But his day was not our day,
And now he sleeps at Porta Nuova, drinks.
In such a night as this
Someone stretches out next to a woman
And feels he no longer has weight,
His tomorrows no longer have weight.
It's today that counts and not tomorrow,
And the flow of time pauses briefly.
In such a night as this
Witches used to choose hemlock and hellebore
To pick by the light of the moon
And cook in their kitchens.
In such a night as this
There's a transvestite on Corso Matteotti
Who would give a kidney and a lung
To grow hollow and become a woman.

                In such a night as this
There are seven young men in white lab coats,
Four of them smoking pipes.
They are designing a very long channel
In which to unite a bundle of protons
Almost as swift as light.
If they succeed, the world will blow up.
                In such a night as this,
A poet strains his bow, searching for a word
That can contain the typhoon's force,
The secrets of blood and seed.

Previously Uncollected Poems

Translated by Ruth Feldman

'Gedale's Song'

Do you recognize us? We are the ghetto sheep,
Shorn for a thousand years, resigned to injury.
We are the tailors, the copyists, and the cantors
Withered in the shadow of the Cross.
Now we know the forest paths,
We have learned to shoot and we're right on target.
 If I am not for myself, who will be for me?
 If not like this, how? And if not now, when?
Our brothers have risen to the sky
Through the ovens of Sobibór and Treblinka,
They have dug themselves a grave in the air.
Only we few have survived
For the honor of our submerged people,
For revenge and witnessing.
 If I am not for myself, who will be for me?
 If not like this, how? And if not now, when?
We are the sons of David, and the stubborn ones of
 Massada.
Each of us carries in his pocket the stone
That shattered Goliath's forehead.
Brothers, away from the Europe of graves:
We will climb together toward the land
Where we shall be men among other men.
 If I am not for myself, who will be for me?
 If not like this, how? And if not now, when?

Decathlon Man

Believe me, the marathon is nothing,
Neither are the hammer and the weights: no single
 contest
Can compare with our ordeal.
I won, yes: I'm more famous today than yesterday,
But a lot older, and worn out.
I ran the four hundred like a hawk,
Without pity for the runner just behind me.
Who was he? No one in particular, a novice,
Never seen before,
A poor Third World wretch,
But the man running beside you is always a monster.
I broke his back, the way I wanted to;
Relishing his agony, I didn't feel my own.
As for the pole-vault, that was less easy,
But luckily for me the judges
Didn't notice my trick
And I did the five metres well.
In the case of the javelin – that's my secret:
You don't have to hurl it against the sky.
The sky is empty: why would you want to run it
 through?
All you need do is picture, at the far end of the meadow,
The man or woman you want dead
And the javelin will turn into a weapon.
It will scent blood, and will fly farther.
I wouldn't know what to say about the fifteen hundred;
I ran it in a state of dizziness
And with cramps, determined, desperate,
Terrified by the convulsive drumbeat of my heart.

I won, but it cost me a lot.
Afterward the discus was lead-heavy
And fell out of my hand, slippery
With my broken veteran's sweat.
They booed me from the sidelines;
Don't think I didn't hear it.
But what do you people require of us?
What more can you demand?
To take off into the air?
Compose a poem in Sanskrit?
Arrive at the end of *pi greco*?
Console the sorrowful?
Operate by compassion's rules?

4 SEPTEMBER 1984

Dust

How much dust settles
On the nervous tissue of a life?
Dust has neither weight nor sound,
Color nor aim: it veils, erases,
Obliterates, hides and paralyzes.
It doesn't kill. It extinguishes.
Isn't dead but sleeps.
It harbors millenial spores
Teeming with future harm.
Tiny chrysalids waiting
To split, decompose, break down:
Pure confused indefinite ambush
Ready for the coming assault,
Impotences that will become potent
At the sounding of a silent signal.
But it also harbors various seeds,
Half-drowsy ones that will grow into ideas,
Each one close-packed with an unforeseen
Universe, new, lovely and strange.
Therefore respect and fear
This gray and formless mantle:
It contains evil and good,
Danger, and many written things.

29 SEPTEMBER 1984

[78]

A Valley

There is a valley which only I know.
It's not reached easily.
There are crags at the entrance,
Thickets and secret fords and rushing waters,
And the paths are reduced to faint traces.
Most atlases don't know about it:
I found the way in by myself.
It took me years,
Making mistakes, as often happens,
But it wasn't wasted time.
I don't know who was there before me:
One person, several, none;
It doesn't matter.
There are marks on the slabs of rock,
Some beautiful, all mysterious;
Some certainly not made by human hands.
Toward the bottom there are beech trees and birches;
Up above, larches and firs,
Always sparser, tormented by the wind
That carries off their pollen in the spring
When the first marmots wake.
Still higher there are seven lakes
Of unpolluted water,
Limpid, dark, icy and very deep.
At this elevation, the local plants
Give out, but almost on the pass
There is a sturdy solitary tree,
Thriving and evergreen,
Which no one has ever named:
Maybe it's the one mentioned in Genesis.

It blossoms and bears fruit in every season,
Even when snow burdens its branches.
There are no others of its kind: it fertilizes itself.
Its trunk bears old wounds
From which a bittersweet
Resin oozes, bearer of oblivion.

29 OCTOBER 1984

Unresolved Burdens

I wouldn't want to upset the universe.
I'd like, if possible,
To cross the border silently,
With the light step of a smuggler.
The way one slips away from a party.
To stop without a screech
The lungs' obstinate piston,
And say to the dear heart,
That mediocre musician without rhythm:
'After two, six billion beats
You must be tired too, so thanks, enough.'
If it were possible, as I was saying,
If it were not for those who will remain,
The work left truncated
(Every life is truncated),
The world's turns and its wounds;
If it were not for the unresolved burdens,
The debts incurred earlier on,
The old unavoidable obligations.

10 DECEMBER 1984

Song of Those Who Died in Vain

Sit down and bargain
All you like, grizzled old foxes.
We'll wall you up in a splendid palace
With food, wine, good beds and a good fire
Provided that you discuss, negotiate
For our and your children's lives.
May all the wisdom of the universe
Converge to bless your minds
And guide you in the maze.
But outside in the cold we will be waiting for you,
The army of those who died in vain,
We of the Marne, of Montecassino,
Treblinka, Dresden and Hiroshima.
And with us will be
The leprous and the people with trachoma,
The Disappeared Ones of Buenos Aires,
Dead Cambodians and dying Ethiopians,
The Prague negotiators,
The bled-dry of Calcutta,
The innocents slaughtered in Bologna.
Heaven help you if you come out disagreeing:
You'll be clutched tight in our embrace.
We are invincible because we are the conquered,
Invulnerable because already dead;
We laugh at your missiles.
Sit down and bargain
Until your tongues are dry.
If the havoc and the shame continue
We'll drown you in our putrefaction.

14 JANUARY 1985

[82]

The Thaw

When all the snow has melted
We'll go to look for the old path,
The one with brambles growing over it
Behind the monastery wall.
Everything will be the way it used to be.

On both sides, among the crowding heather
We'll rediscover certain stunted grasses
Whose name I never could remember for you;
It comes back to me every Friday
But by Saturday it's forgotten.
I'm told they're rare,
A good remedy for melancholy.

The ferns on the edges of the path
Are delicate as infants:
They barely poke out of the ground,
Curled up in spirals, and yet
They're ready for their loves already,
Alternating and green, more intricate than ours.

Their seeds eat away the brakes,
Small males and females,
In the rusty spore-sacs.
They'll burst forth at the first rain,
Swimming in the first drop,
Wilful and quick. Long live the bridal pairs!

We're tired of winter. The ice's
Bite has left its mark
On flesh, mind, mud and wood.
Let the thaw come, and let it melt
The memory of last year's snow.

Samson

Son of a sterile mother
I too was announced
By a messenger with an awesome face.
I was a child of the Sun, a sun myself;
I had the Sun's strength
Compressed into my bull's loins.
I, sun and wild beast,
Have killed my enemies in the thousands,
Broken down doors and burst chains,
Ravaged women and set fire to harvests,
Until a Philistine Delilah
Cropped my hair and my stamina,
Extinguished my eyes' light.
There is no struggling against the dark.
My hair grew back
And so did my brute force.
Not the desire to live.

Delilah

Samson of Tinnata, the rebel,
Mountain-splitting Jew,
Was, in my delicate hands,
Soft as potter's clay.
It was child's play to wrest the secret
Of his much-vaunted strength.
With praise and blandishments
I lulled him to sleep in my lap,
Still full of his foreign seed,
Blinded him, cut off his hair,
Destroying the power of his loins.
My rage and wantonness
Have never found so much peace
As on the day when I saw him in chains –
Not when I felt him penetrate me.
Now let him meet his fate. What do I care?

5 APRIL 1985

Airport

It was a sampling of humanity in transit,
As though chosen at random
To be submitted to a foreign buyer:
Rich and poor, fat and lean,
Indians, blacks, whites, invalids, infants.
What does humanity do in transit?
Nothing of much account.
It chatters, sleeps, puffs smoke in armchairs.
What will the buyer say? What will he offer
For that seventy-year-old woman in tights?
The eight people uttering banalities?
Grandparents, mothers, grand- and great-grandchildren?
For those obese mushrooms
Who barely squeeze between the chair-arms?
For the two of us, tired of foreign words?

We're leaving. The great cavernous bird
Sucks us all up every which way:
We cross the Acheron
Through the telescopic tube.
The plane taxis, accelerates, gains power,
Takes off and in a moment
Rises into the sky
Body and soul: our bodies and souls.
Are we worthy of Assumption?

Now it flies into purple twilight
Above the ice of nameless seas,
Or over a dark cloak of clouds,
As if this planet of ours
Had veiled its face in shame.
Then it flies with muffled thumps
As though someone were driving so many piles
Into the bottom of the Stygian swamp;
Later instead, along soft
Smooth tracks of air.
The night is sleepless but short
As no night has ever been,
Light and gay as a first night.

At Malapensa, Lisa, her face
Keen and shining, was waiting for us.
I don't believe it was a useless trip.

29 MAY 1985

[88]

On Trial

'My name? Alex Zink.' 'Where were you born?'
'In Nuremberg, that illustrious ancient city.
Rightly famous, honest judge.
First, because certain laws were passed there
That are of no interest here.
Second, for a debatable trial.
Third, because the best toys
In the whole world are produced there.'
'Tell me how you lived,
And don't lie. It would be useless here.'
'I was hardworking, Your Honor.
Stone on top of stone, *mark* after *mark*,
I founded a model industry.
The best buckram, the finest felt
Were made by the Zink Company.
I was a humane and diligent boss:
Honest prices, generous salaries,
Never a complaint from my customers.
And above all, as I was telling you,
The best felt produced in Europe.'
'Did you use good wool?'
'Extraordinary wool, Your Honor,
Loose or in braids,
Wool of which I had the monopoly.
Black wool and chestnut, tawny and blonde;
More often gray or white.'
'From what flocks?'
'I don't know. It didn't interest me;
I paid for it in cash.'
'Tell me: have your dreams been tranquil?'

[89]

'Usually yes, judge.
Though sometimes in my dreams
I've heard grieving ghosts groan.'
'Weaver, stand down.'

19 JULY 1985

Thieves

They come at night, like wisps of fog,
Often in full daylight too.
Unnoticed, they filter through
Cracks and keyholes,
Noiselessly, leaving no trace,
No broken locks, and no disorder.
They are the thieves of time,
Fluid and sticky like leeches:
They drink your time and spit it out
The way you'd toss away trash.
You've never seen them face to face. Do they have faces?
Lips and tongue – yes, certainly
And tiny pointed teeth.
They suck without provoking pain,
Leave only a livid scar.

14 OCTOBER 1985

[91]

To My Friends

Dear friends, and here I say friends
In the broad sense of the word:
Wife, sister, associates, relatives,
Schoolmates of both sexes,
People seen only once
Or frequented all my life;
Provided that between us, for at least a moment,
A line has been stretched,
A well-defined bond.

I speak for you, companions of a crowded
Road, not without its difficulties,
And for you too, who have lost
Soul, courage, the desire to live;
Or no one, or someone, or perhaps only one person, or
    you
Who are reading me: remember the time
Before the wax hardened,
When everyone was like a seal.
Each of us bears the imprint
Of a friend met along the way;
In each the trace of each.
For good or evil
In wisdom or in folly
Everyone stamped by everyone.

Now that time crowds in
And the undertakings are finished,
To all of you the humble wish
That autumn will be long and mild.

16 DECEMBER 1985

Proxy

Don't be afraid if the work is hard:
You who are less tired are needed.
Since your senses are fine-tuned, you hear
The hollow sound under your feet.
Consider our mistakes again:
We have also had among us
Someone who set about searching blindly
The way a blindfolded man repeats an outline,
Someone who set sail like the pirates,
And someone who tried his very best.
Help, insecure one. Try, though you're insecure,
Because you're insecure. See
If you can repress the annoyance and disgust
Of our doubts and certainties.
Never have we been so rich and yet
We live in the midst of embalmed monsters,
Other monsters obscenely alive.
Don't be dismayed by the rubble,
Or the stench of refuse dumps: we
Cleared them up with our bare hands
In the years when we were your age.
Continue the race, as best you can. We have
Combed the comets' mane,
Deciphered the secrets of origins,
Trampled the moon's sand,
Built Auschwitz and destroyed Hiroshima.
See: we have not remained inactive.
Take up the cause, perplexed one;
Don't call us teachers.

24 JUNE 1986

[94]

August

Who stays in the city in August?
Only the poor and the mad,
Forgotten little old ladies,
Pensioners with their little dogs,
Thieves, some gentlemen and the cats.
Through the deserted streets
You hear a continual tapping of heels,
See women with plastic bags
In the streak of shade along the walls.
Under the fountain with its small tower
In the pool green with algae
There's a middle-aged naiad
About four inches long
With nothing on but a brassière.
A few yards farther on,
Despite the well-known prohibition,
The begging pigeons
Surround you in a flock
And steal the bread out of your hand.
Rustling in the sky, in weary flight,
You hear the noontime demon.

22 JULY 1986

[95]

The Fly

I am the only one here; this
Is a clean hospital.
I am the messenger.
For me there are no closed doors,
And there's always a window,
A crack, a keyhole.
I find plenty of food,
Left by the satiated
And those who can no longer eat.
        I draw nourishment too
From discarded drugs,
Since nothing harms me,
Everything feeds, strengthens and serves me:
Noble and ignoble matter,
Blood, pus, kitchen waste.
I transform everything into flight energy;
My function urges me on.
I am the last one to kiss the burnt lips
Of the dying and the doomed.
I am important. My monotonous
Murmur, annoying and senseless,
Repeats the only message of the world
To those who cross the threshold:
        I am the mistress here,
        The only free one, healthy and unconstrained.

31 AUGUST 1986

The Dromedary

What's the use of so many quarrels, lawsuits and wars?
You need only imitate me.
No water? I go without it,
Careful only not to waste breath.
No food? I tap my hump.
When times are favorable,
Grow one yourselves.
And if my hump's gone soft
A little brushwood and straw suffice me.
Green grass is vanity and lust.
I have an ugly voice? I'm almost always mute;
If I do bellow, nobody hears me.
I'm homely? I please my mate.
Our females look for solid qualities
And give the best milk that exists.
Try asking as much from yours.
Yes, I'm a servant, but the desert is mine;
There is no servant without his own kingdom.
Mine is desolation.
It is limitless.

24 NOVEMBER 1986

Almanac

The indifferent rivers
Will keep on flowing to the sea
Or ruinously overflowing dikes,
Ancient handiwork of determined men.
The glaciers will continue to grate,
Smoothing what lies beneath them,
Or suddenly fall headlong,
Cutting short fir trees' lives.
The sea, captive between
Two continents, will go on struggling,
Always miserly with its riches.
Sun, stars, planets and comets
Will continue on their course.
Earth too will fear the immutable
Laws of the universe.
Not us. We, rebellious offspring
With great brainpower, little sense,
Will destroy, defile,
Always more feverishly.
Very soon we will extend the desert
Into the Amazon forests,
Into the living heart of our cities,
Into our very hearts.

2 JANUARY 1987

[98]

Notes

5 'Buna' – the name of the factory in the concentration camp Buna-Monowitz, an Auschwitz subsidiary, in which Levi worked for a time during his imprisonment.

6 'Singing' – cf. Siegfried Sassoon, 'Everyone Sang'.

7 '25 February 1944' – cf. *Inferno*, Canto III, 1. 57; *Purgatorio*, Canto V, 1. 134; and T. S. Eliot, *The Waste Land*: 'I had not thought death had undone so many.'

9 'Shemà' – means 'Hear!' in Hebrew. It is the first word of the fundamental prayer of Judaism, in which the unity of God is affirmed. Some lines of this poem are paraphrases.

10 'Reveille' – 'Wstawać' means 'Get up!' in Polish.

12 'Another Monday' – for the last line cf. *Vita Nuova*, Canto XXVI, 'Tanto gentile . . .'

14 '*Ostjuden*' – in National Socialist Germany this was the official term for Polish and Russian Jews.

15 'Sunset at Fòssoli' – cf. *Catulli Liber* 5, 4. At Fòssoli, near Carpo, was the holding and sorting camp for the prisoners destined for deportation.

16 '11 February 1946' – this poem did not form part of the original volume which we published under the title *Shemà*, or the corresponding Italian edition, *L'osteria di Brema*, published by Vanni Scheiwiller. Primo Levi added it when he incorporated the earlier book into *Ad ora incerta*.

19 'Avigliana' – l. 15: Levi's wife's name is Lucia; fireflies are 'lucciole' in Italian.

22 'The Crow's Song II' – cf. T. S. Eliot, 'The Hollow Men': 'This is the way the world ends/Not with a bang but a whimper.'

25 'Landing' – cf. H. Heine, *Buch der Lieder*, 'Die Nordsee', II Zyklus, no. 9: 'Glücklich der Mann, der den Hafen erreicht hat . . .'

26 'Lilith' – for the legends relative to Lilith, see the story by the same name in Primo Levi's collection *Lilít e altri racconti*, Einaudi, 1981; English translation *Moments of Reprieve*, Summit Books, Inc./Simon & Schuster, New York, 1986, and Michael Joseph Ltd, London, 1986.

l. 13: actually three Hebrew letters – Shin, Daleth, Yod – comprising 'Shaddai', an ancient name for God. Observant Italian mothers suspend these medallions over their babies' beds. In the Cabbalist tradition still strong in many Mediterranean and Oriental Jewish communities, 'Shaddai' is often engraved on signet rings and other pieces of personal jewelry that are worn as protection against the Evil Eye.

27 'In the Beginning' – 'Bereshìd', in the beginning, is the first word of the Holy Scriptures. On Big Bang, which is alluded to here, see, for example, the *Scientific American* of June 1970.

29 'The Black Stars' – cf. *Scientific American*, December 1974.

30 'Leavetaking' – 'nebbich' is Yiddish for foolish, useless, inept.

33 'Pliny' – Pliny the Elder died in AD 79 from having gone too close to Vesuvius in the course of the eruption that destroyed Pompeii.

42 '12 July 1980' – the sixtieth birthday of Levi's wife.

43 'Dark Band' – cf. *Purgatorio*, Canto XXVI, 1. 34.

46 'Voices' – cf. F. Villon, *Le Testament*, Stanza CLIX, 1. 1720.

48 'Partisan' – the Italian title 'Partigia' is a Piedmontese abbreviation (like 'burgu' for 'borghese', 'Juve' for 'Juventus', 'prepu' for 'prepotente', 'cumenda' for 'commendatore', etc.) to designate a partisan, with the connotation of one who is open-minded, decisive, able. 'INPS': National Institute of Social Security.

51 'Passover' – this poem contains various quotations from the traditional Seder ritual of the Jewish Passover. A sweet chopped apple mixture symbolizes the mortar ('malta' in Italian) used by Jewish slave laborers in the building of the Pharaohs' huge monuments.

54 'Old Mole' – cf. *Hamlet*, Act I, Scene 5: 'old mole'.

58 'Nachtwache' – this means 'night watchman' in German. It was a technical concentration-camp term. The first line is from Isaiah, 21, 11.

60 'Pearl Oyster' – the Meleagrina, pearl-bearing oyster, is a different species from the common edible one.

63 'Flight' – cf. T. S. Eliot, *The Waste Land*, 1. 332: 'Rock and no water and the sandy road.'

64 'The Survivor' – cf. S. T. Coleridge, *The Rime of the Ancient Mariner*, 1. 582, and *Inferno*, Canto XXXIII, 1, 141: 'e mangia e bee e dorme e veste panni.'

65 'The Elephant' – the 'bold blind man' is Hannibal who, according to tradition, contracted an eye disease during his crossing of the Alps.

67 'Sidereus Nuncius' – Galileo saw three bodies of Saturn because of imperfections in his spyglass.

68 'Give Us' – a Nagant is a kind of gun.

71 'Memorandum Book' – ('Agenda' in Italian) was not in the Garzanti volume *Ad ora incerta*. It was sent to me by Primo Levi in a letter, and he approved the translation and its inclusion. R. F.

73 'Gedale's Song', originally untitled, is taken from Primo Levi's novel *Se Non Ora, Quando?* in which Gedale, a partisan leader, attributes the words of his song (he says the tune keeps changing) to a Martin Fontasch, who was with him in the Kossovo ghetto. The German who killed him was a music-lover and allowed Fontasch one last wish, provided it was

reasonable. Fontasch asked to be allowed to compose one last song. Gedale says the words came into his hands via a Russian who was in the cell next to Fontasch.

Index of titles